PRAISE FOR *OIL COURSES*

"'How many steps between your family and an oil well?' This is a question asked by Carolyn Williams-Noren in the plainly spoken yet deeply complicated *Oil Courses.* Her own answer is one she's struggled with, especially as her father 'earned a living' in the drilling industry and with her own experience as a young person at Endicott, an entirely human-made island of 45 acres built for offshore oil production. Yet each of these carefully wrought poems offers an answer, not only exploring the ethics of her own complicity but also demonstrating just how we're all tangled into petroleum's sticky web of exploitation. Painfully reckoning with our whale-slaughtering past as well as with an uncertain future in which so much of the weather was once simply taken for granted as 'ordinary,' these poems don't simply emote—they make a careful and measured study to gain perspective. Showing just how the word *hypocrite* is 'always ready to burn the veins,' this steadfast debut doesn't offer solutions, no. It does something quite important during this time of climate crisis: it complicates—and humanizes—the question of how we got here in the first place."—**Nickole Brown,** author of *To Those Who Were Our First Gods* and *The Donkey Elegies*

"*Oil Courses* is learned in loving ways. Its wisdom arrives from multiple disciplines and spans across generations. Each poem is sourced by Carolyn Williams-Noren's resilient curiosity and the kind of attention that can only result from deep yearning—for knowledge, for understanding, for different, for better. That same desire is evident in the care Williams-Noren takes to convey what she has come to understand from a lifetime of studious inquiry. On every page, *Oil Courses* engages and entertains; it's a dazzling and memorable debut."—**Michael Kleber-Diggs,** author of *Worldly Things*

OIL COURSES

Wick Poetry First Book Series

DAVID HASSLER, EDITOR

Oil Courses by Carolyn Williams-Noren	Pádraig Ó Tuama, Judge
The Deep Blue of Neptune by Terry Belew	Alison Hawthorne Deming, Judge
Opium and Ambergris by Colin Dekeersgieter	Marilyn Chin, Judge
Fraternal Light: On Painting While Black by Arlene Keizer	Cornelius Eady, Judge
Sister Tongue زبان خواهر by Farnaz Fatemi	Tracy K. Smith, Judge
How Blood Works by Ellene Glenn Moore	Richard Blanco, Judge
On This Side of the Desert by Alfredo Aguilar	Natalie Diaz, Judge
The Many Names for Mother by Julia Kolchinsky Dasbach	Ellen Bass, Judge
Fugue Figure by Michael McKee Green	Khaled Mattawa, Judge
Even Years by Christine Gosnay	Angie Estes, Judge
hover over her by Leah Poole Osowski	Adrian Matejka, Judge
Translation by Matthew Minicucci	Jane Hirshfield, Judge
The Spectral Wilderness by Oliver Bendorf	Mark Doty, Judge
The Dead Eat Everything by Michael Mlekoday	Dorianne Laux, Judge
Wet by Carolyn Creedon	Edward Hirsch, Judge
The Local World by Mira Rosenthal	Maggie Anderson, Judge

MAGGIE ANDERSON, EDITOR EMERITA

Visible Heavens by Joanna Solfrian	Naomi Shihab Nye, Judge
The Infirmary by Edward Micus	Stephen Dunn, Judge
Far from Algiers by Djelloul Marbrook	Toi Derricotte, Judge
Constituents of Matter by Anna Leahy	Alberto Rios, Judge
Intaglio by Ariana-Sophia M. Kartsonis	Eleanor Wilner, Judge
Trying to Speak by Anele Rubin	Philip Levine, Judge
Rooms and Fields: Dramatic Monologues from the War in Bosnia by Lee Peterson	Jean Valentine, Judge
The Drowned Girl by Eve Alexandra	C. K. Williams, Judge
Back Through Interruption by Kate Northrop	Lynn Emanuel, Judge
Paper Cathedrals by Morri Creech	Li-Young Lee, Judge
The Gospel of Barbecue by Honorée Fanonne Jeffers	Lucille Clifton, Judge
Beyond the Velvet Curtain by Karen Kovacik	Henry Taylor, Judge
The Apprentice of Fever by Richard Tayson	Marilyn Hacker, Judge

Oil Courses

Poems by

Carolyn Williams-Noren

The Kent State University Press

Kent, Ohio

Library of Congress Catalog Card Number 2026016944
ISBN 978-1-60635-511-4 (Paper)
ISBN 978-1-63101-587-8 (ePub)

The Wick Poetry Series is sponsored by the Stan and Tom Wick Poetry Center and the Department of English at Kent State University.

The manufacturer's authorized representative in the EU for product safety is Mare Nostrum Group B.V., Mauritskade 21D, 1091 GC Amsterdam, The Netherlands, email gpsr@mare-nostrum.co.uk.

LIBRARY OF CONGRESS CATALOGING-IN-PUBLICATION DATA
Names: Williams-Noren, Carolyn author
Title: Oil courses / poems by Carolyn Williams-Noren.
Description: Kent, Ohio : The Kent State University Press, 2026. | Series: Wick poetry first book
Identifiers: LCCN 2026016944 | ISBN 9781606355114 paperback | ISBN 9781631015878 epub
Subjects: LCGFT: Poetry
Classification: LCC PS3623.I56667 O45 2026
LC record available at https://lccn.loc.gov/2026016944

In this way / we gradually learned about our country.
—Ruth Stone, "American Milk"

What of ours is our own?
—Sarah Vap, *Winter*

I learn by going where I have to go.
—Theodore Roethke, "The Waking"

CONTENTS

The table of contents for Carolyn Williams-Noren's *Oil Courses* reads like an assemblage of homework assignments: history, physics, assignment, law, economics, art, essay, music, and research. Each title comes with a timestamp too: 1991, 1985, Now, and 2021. Reading the sequence we get to know some of the stages of the poet's life—she was younger than 16 in 1985, worked on Endicott Island in 1993, and so on.

Throughout it all: oil courses. Oil from the petroleum industry she learnt to conceal in conversations with friends at college. Is the *courses* of the title a verb or a noun? Yes. When it's a noun, the oil courses teach about illusion, hypocrisy, employment, culture, seizure, chosen ignorance, and yearned-for change. When it's a verb, the oil courses through the poet's body like some additional substance. In "Economics I [1985]," we hear a young speaker repeat—verbatim, it seems—a line from home where if your food comes from the store and the petrol used in the vehicle that brought the food to the store, and from the store to your home, then "How can you criticize / what you're made of, it's / like complaining about air." But later ("English I [1991]"), two changes are evident: the speaker's critique of the oil industry that employs her father in Alaska has risen to the surface; and a critique of the culture—whether of the workers, or Petroleum Wives gathered in a "Captain Cook / ballroom" to hear an adolescent read an essay—has also been unearthed.

Did I say two changes? No, I meant three. The speaker is now a writer: she's reciting from the stage because she's won a competition for an essay on "What Petroleum Means / to Me." "The point was *don't do it*," she says, but it seems her audience and judges have not cottoned on to the message she's traced from depleting resources, and the exploitation of Indigenous people and communities. In a later poem, looking at a pen—made from byproducts of the petroleum industry—she writes, "And now this pen will survive / me." What is this? It is a poet thinking of the futurity of her writing. What is this? It is a poet thinking of the futurity of her planet. What is this? It is a poet.

These are poems of action, character, furniture, event, memory, and locale. Following Stanley Kunitz's famous induction to *finish with an image; don't explain it,* Williams-Noren sometimes employs shocking endings:

Later that summer, or maybe
another summer, a bear killed someone
right there—an old woman jogging up the trail.

Life and death: in Alaska, in Minneapolis where she now lives, between human and animal; between humans and the energy industry; between humans and our world.

A poem is not a moral declaration, and also, a poem is an act of making from a person, a person who has moral reckonings, curiosities, regrets, and messages. Tension is evident in her line breaks, as well as in the artistic integrity of those same lines. In "Assignment [Now]" we hear:

How to hear a father say
I sacrificed and say
thank you. And
I reject it. And *I'm*
made of it and *stop*

In his journal, Jack Kerouac wrote, "I wonder why our life must quiver between beauty and guilt, consummation and sadness, desire and regret, immortality and tattered moments unknowable, truth and beautiful meaningful lies." Carolyn Williams-Noren's poems chart similar concerns. In "Geography IX [1993]," she reflects that a job she had on Endicott Island provided for her: "The money I made / would buy books, books I still own, / and ten-dollar pizza every time / I craved it, through the rest / of college. I wouldn't go back." She isn't using declamation as a way of manufacturing moral or physical distance. Rather, she implies herself, exploring the etymological relationships of that word in "English II [Now]." Guilt is an experience, but crucially, in her work, it is a place too. As the book reaches its end, we hear how, speaking for the "first time since 1992, with Thomas Williams, no relation," she hears him say:

I definitely live with a deep sense of hypocrisy every day
of my life, and when I hear these easy words
I feel closer to home than I've been in a long time.

Oil courses through her characters, her speaker, her artistic and political imagination, and—in these poems, deft in voice, form, punch, and music—through us too.

Pádraig Ó Tuama
New York City, January 2026

1983–1992: Anchorage
1993: Endicott Island
2018–Now: Minneapolis

HISTORY III [2018]

After we order dinner, my dad in a voice
he especially wants my daughters to hear:
Before we started taking oil out of the ground, we
hunted whales. We killed them. Thousands. For
light. It's as bad as the cooking show I chose

last night for all of us, not expecting a side of hog
hung on a hook, butcher in a white coat, cutting
skin & bone & flesh like butter, meat so oddly
dry, so pale. He must have told me this same story
years ago. And still my best question is *Everywhere?*

Why do I go with him toward the history of whaling?
Not just Inuit? Not just those stone lamps? This is over
a smorgasbord of terrine and chicken liver paste, dabs
I mete onto little rounds of bread for the girls to try.
All over the world *they were using whale oil for light?*

I don't know why I think this is the way. He says, *We have*
a lamp with a glass chimney. We have it at home. Whales
dying. For light. My daughters listen. I do remember
hearing this, about whales. I remember it stopping

what tried to rise in me. The other way
is *But that doesn't justify,* and then *Never said* and
Would you rather we'd. Now the quiet that says
nobody's willing. My husband silent. My mother

silent until Dad says, *They were killing whales all the time*
anyway, for ambergris to make perfume (who can argue
with someone who remembers ambergris?) and Mom
says, *And for corsets. They used whale bones for*
corsets. To my daughters: *To hold your waist in.* One
daughter: *I thought corsets were lacy. How could bones—*
I start to explain, then a woman whose face I forget
right away arrives with pasta, and my mom is still
mimicking squeezing her waist, cheeks sucked in.

I said at a dorm-room party, just like
anybody would talk about the weather,
My dad works for an oil company, and
the circle tilted a degree, then spun away.

The boy I'd come with said, *Don't say that*
like that, and I said, *Like what?* And he said,
Like there's nothing wrong. It was good
advice. I learned a movement that said, *Not*
mine. Eyes to an upper corner. A sideways
motion. A shoulder, sometimes. I said *oil*

company because nobody in Minnesota
knew BP before the yellow-and-green
sunflower logo reached the middle
of the continent. But then one acquaintance
after another looked at me knowingly and said,
Oh—Exxon? Like I'd tried to hide my relation

to that familiar villain. So then for a while
it was *British Petroleum.* And later I just said
BP, with the expression, and let people go
right to Deepwater Horizon. Then time

went by and I stayed still, and nobody
asked anymore *Where are you from*
or *What did your parents do*
there, and for a long time
I haven't had to say it at all, and it's easy
to think I might never be asked to again.

GEOGRAPHY I [1983]

The winter sunrise tore off the red edge
of the mountains at 10 a.m. and that
was ordinary. Snow piled along the street
and in spring meltwater ran hidden
through its tunnels down the hill and
that was ordinary. Rhubarb grew

thick as my wrist, chickweed
all through the lawn, lawns
bright green and that too

and beyond them woods,
between them woods
of mosquitoes, fireweed, spruce, spruce,
birch, lichen on rocks, lichen
on trunks and branches and
hung on twigs, frazzled wool. All this

was ordinary. The black spruce along
Abbott, hunched together, hundreds,
snow-burdened, every winter day.

In winter, it was sunrise or sunset
more often than not. In fall,
the birches turned yellow
and the spruce stayed green
and it rained. In summer, I might
run barefoot up the street
at midnight. In spring,
water, water. On every side,

mountains. West, the inlet.
The story was you couldn't walk
on the flats; the mud would soften
as the tide came up, suck you in.
A man was pulled out by helicopters,
torn in half instead of rescued.

I first heard that in the car of the realtor
who for three whole days drove us
to houses whose walls were textured like maps of

continents and ocean and whose entryways
led up and down at once.
Houses with intercoms, houses
I'd think of later when friends' dads
were said to be *in construction,* houses with
machines to squeeze garbage down small,
grind garbage and send it down the sink.
Nubbly white ceilings, windows
that opened on diamond-shaped
hinges, rooms with names—foyer,
den, master bath, crawlspace,
cold floors on cement slabs,
in each room a little portal

that opened, caused a vacuum
somewhere in the house
to start its pull. You could attach
a hose, a brush, and clean the floor, or

you could place your palm across that hole
and feel it seal, feel the machine believe
your hand was the cover swinging shut
and turn off. All this, I knew, was ordinary.

SCIENCE FAIR II [1987]

One year was thickness—I learned
it was called viscosity. How fast
a liquid was willing to change
its shape. My experiment wouldn't
discover anything new. How thick
was one motor oil or another in the cold
or in the heat? It was written already
on every can—numbers, *W*'s,
dashes. But on the kitchen floor
a paint tray, like for a roller brush,
the funnel, its opening, its inside
marked with measurements—
I counted milliliters per second—
pour to the line, hold the hole
with my finger, stopwatch—

big grey buttons and how long
it took to empty. Dovetailed
red and blue *V* of Valvoline. Green
and the wavy-tailed *Q* of
Quaker State. Some was golden, like
I'd pour on pancakes. Some
was darker—molasses or filth—
the hydrocarbon chain. It started
with molecules, with dinosaurs, and
cleaning up did I pour it
down the sink? I didn't wear
the gloves I was supposed to wear.
Washing the pan, I let oil become
an extra skin—cool, then warmer—
clinging even under the faucet,
even under handfuls of soap.

MATHEMATICS I [1985]

The first time my parents flew to Prudhoe
they came home talking about tundra—
as far as they could see, not a road, not a farm.

Under sixteen weren't allowed on the tour
so we'd stayed all day with neighbors,
me and my brother. *The vastness.* They came home
and explained the word *acre.* They kept
saying *the vastness.* They'd flown over miles

and miles and miles of flat brown-grassy land
holding so many narrow lakes. And sod
over permafrost, over thousands of years, breaks
into polygons—a quilt of them, mud cracks
writ large, horizon to horizon. The land was large,
large and went on forever, would allow anything.

MATHEMATICS II [1985]

Looking back, maybe they were a little
drunk? If they were buzzed they made it look
like elation. Levitation. They mentioned
living on land in the wilderness, then somehow
a sailboat, the wind, the land, unending land.

LITERATURE I [2020]

I remember my mom watching and crying over
Howards End, and not watching, myself, but
instead asking all the obvious questions like

Who's Howard? Decades later, a friend
said she loved the book, and I read it
and fell in love too with the hundred-years-ago women

who talk blithely about the money they live on—
where it comes from—who fret about
what the rubber industry does to people

and how much they profit from it, talk about
a man so focused that he can't see
at all, and yet they all partake. Now I watch the show

evenings on the couch with Anders, fed and clothed
by geology and editing (but also on this broken-
promise land in the middle of the continent

and by the light of god-knows-what) and add
to my list of loves the mouth of Helen
and the grey sweater with blue-and-white trim

worn by the odd androgynous Tibby. I feel related to
Mr. Wilcox, whose office wall has a map of Africa
in ebony and gold like (I check the book) *a whale*

marked out for blubber. Draw the check, only
connect. Anders likes the show but says, *I wonder*
what it means. And he says it seems so current

he doubts it's all in a book from the nineteen-teens.
But it is, all written just like now: the protein restaurant,
these pale people, their guilt, their continuance.

THEORY [NOW]

When I was very small I asked my dad whether he
knew *everything,* and when he said he didn't,
I didn't believe him. From his answer—that we learn

all our lives, every day, but *nobody* knows everything
(to which I asked, *Not even God?* and he,
an agnostic at most, capitulated weakly)—

I gathered that the oldest people know the most,
but not as much as dead people, who probably *do*
know everything. By *know* I meant be able to answer

questions, all of the questions: What is milk made of,
how do our bones grow, why is the sun hot? By *God*
I meant, probably, a reason for things, or a love

without the fickleness or contingency of the human, without
misunderstanding. All to say that *knowing*
became a goal of mine, even then, the desire to be asked

and to answer. My aunt posted on Facebook, with no
preamble besides a blue link to my dad's name,
an article with the title "Rates of Parkinson's Disease

Are Exploding: A Common Chemical May Be to Blame."
The chemical is a degreaser, one I don't know
for sure is used in the oil industry, but I do remember

the gallons of solvents stocked in the warehouse—
sandy orange, luminous green, clear and thin as water.

ART II [1991]

Madame Collins taught French, and also Watercolor Painting
I and II, and after school and without permission,
before pinning our paintings to the corkboard, she'd

lay over each a few careful lines: bring a jaw into
proportion, eyelid edge into relief. Leaf shadow
brighter, branch more smooth. She was French

but born in Algeria. One boy knew her story already
and told it, laughing. He mouthed, *They ran,* and
pantomimed a slow-mo sprint, invisible valise in each hand.
Obviously, I thought. *Obviously the French didn't belong*

in that country they tried to take. Madame Collins
explained in the middle of Wednesday vocabulaire
the word *Pieds-Noirs: They were forced to leave,* she
said, then *Where were we supposed to go? It was our*
home. Our parents'. Grandparents'. Her voice, and

my surprise. That mind of the classroom, the mind
I held, that knew her to be wrong but wouldn't
understand itself the same. Even though we were also
laid across what we called home, and felt ourselves temporary

without words for it, inch of lakewater afternoon-warm, thin.
The mind that watched on the A/V cart TV, lights out,
a movie about that battle, catching not a word of the French
and feeling no kinship, no unease. I wasn't the first to notice

Madame Collins behind the last row of desks
sniffling quietly. I heard some boys snickering,
then Charlotte, whose last name was also Collins

but no relation, Charlotte from Alabama, shushed them,
then softly patted the teacher's shoulder, then
the rest of us in that dim room started to see.

GEOGRAPHY III [1984]

We all knew, had known. We knew
that carbon dioxide in air
would hold in heat like
greenhouse glass. We knew
there was no door to open. Knew
that oil carried in a tanker could spill
like oil and coat feathers and
beaks like oil and smother gills
and scales like oil and slick every rock
and pebble like oil and clot otters'
soft insulating fur like oil. Everywhere,
people knew. And yet

in the office obedient men
mostly, and women with broad
padded shoulders, often jars of
candy on their desks, every day
in the cubicles making work the drills
and the pipes and the more or less
cookers that sorted solid from
liquid from gas, who at dinner tables
would explain to their children the well,
the pressure—fist, fist, the job
of bringing it to the surface safely
and through pipelines to ships,
factories, to become fuel or

plastic or, yes, it's even in
lipstick. Visiting the office we were to
stay quiet and not refer
to any funny thing Dad had said
about his cubicle neighbor
peeking up over the partition,
a prairie dog many times an hour
begging for words and distracting

from the work. On one end of each floor,
a small room where a person could pour coffee
into a disposable cup, or eat a small bag of pretzels.

MATHEMATICS III [1993]

In the warehouse I counted
Nomex suits, gloves, latex
and neoprene, all sizes,
bolts, nuts, god knows
what else, pipe fittings
labeled male-male or
female-male, elbows, T's. It was
inventory. I was
in college, a child-of, and two weeks
at a time I was there. Every
building resting on trucked-in gravel
to protect the tundra, and I
slept in a bare room
occupied in other weeks
by some middle-aged engineer
who left nothing behind.
The guy who ran the warehouse,
Will, he drank a six-pack of Pepsi
every day by noon. Brand-new
state-of-the-art barcode
scanner. I wore steel-toed
boots too big and my body
hurt and the hours were so many
hours. The break room,
cocoa powder mixed into
watery coffee, fifteen minutes
twice a day and lunch. I
printed labels, and some things
I wondered if they were too small
to count: nails, screws. Boxes
of 100, sure, but those that
had spilled out into the bin?
To count those? It felt
wrong to spend the time on
fractions of pennies and wrong
to let it be unknown

how many were left.
Some things were too large
to count: pumps and compressors
at the top of the pallet shelves
which one day I climbed, feeling
the most alive all summer,
pulling up like onto a tree branch
twenty feet above the concrete
onto a shelf whose dust
hadn't been touched in years—until
Will yelled at me to get down. *Don't*
count those—with real fear. Will
wasn't really a guy to climb.
I learned from Will to open a box
with one quick slice to the top,
another across the plastic
packing slip pouch, and a firm
pull at each taped-down lid flap.
Upstairs, the floors were made of
metal grid that swayed and made me
seasick after some hours. Some
metals turned my palms
iridescent grey. Part of the job
was to mop filth off the shelves
after counting, then restack
neatly. Rarely, we went
out in the truck. One time
there was a polar bear
on a nearby beach, and we drove
close enough to catch it
in miniature through binoculars.
Some nights I ate dinner with my dad,
and one time he walked me to his desk
in the office wing, let me use
his computer to type an application
to work at a bookstore

back in town. A job I didn't
get. There was never quiet. I never
went into the modules except
once on a tour where I almost
passed out. The noise, I think
and a hard hat, earplugs, the coat
I needed outdoors much too warm.

ENGLISH III [NOW]

If you think of an island as a place
you get to in a boat, Endicott Island
isn't one. The bus from Deadhorse airport
follows the pipelines along the coast, then
onto the causeway. Look out the window
on the north side and it seems like you're
driving on grey ocean. But you're on
a three-mile road, two lanes, two
narrow shoulders, Endicott a knob
at the end, also made of gravel, all built on
gravel that rests on more gravel that rests
on the ocean floor. *Causeway* has nothing
to do with cause and effect. It's not
a road made for a reason, not a company's
invention. Before *causeway,* we said
calciare, meaning to make a road. Before
we said *calciare,* we said *calx,* meaning
lime, like limestone. And *calx* (no relation)
meaning heel. So two people can disagree
like the linguists do about whether *causeway*
is closer to laying down rocks or closer
to heel, closer to shoe, to treading, to
treading until we've made the way firm.

GEOGRAPHY II [1983]

And before Anchorage we lived in
a past that lost everything but
classroom with wooden chairs,
hundred-year-old house, blue paint
peeling, ivy, cherry tree, chestnuts,
sidewalks, crosswalk, lawn in winter,
red tomatoes, drive to the grandparents'.
School where my granddad knew the bell.
And I remembered it like—wood floors,
laurel hedge, apple trees, spring in March,
thin Halloween costumes. In nine years
one single precious snow day.

And we came from a brick road
that woke me up as we rounded
the last corner home, garage
tucked under the house, locust tree's
tiny leaves, wooden fence, sheepdog
lapping up my brother's Ovaltine.
What I'd remember again and again
on purpose was the old school, walking
the back way through the alley. Alleys,
tall trees, orange leaves.

SCIENCE FAIR I [1986]

To write about viscosity, I read
a small book by Isaac Asimov
(a name that impressed my dad)
called *How Did We Find Out*
About Oil? I would have forgotten
all this if first my mom and then I
hadn't kept the report—with its
laminated cover and its title
in bubble letters crowded
against one another, colored
with Mr. Sketch raspberry blue:
Petroleum and Its Viscosity.

I paid attention to Romans, who
soaked pigs in oil and set them
on fire to send into battle. Paid
attention to one-celled creatures
dying in the ocean and instead
of being eaten, sinking, becoming
buried with silt and changing from
whatever one-celled creatures are
to long chains of carbon molecules
hemmed around by hydrogens, a diagram
I xeroxed at the library and glued
to a page without regard for copyright.
How strange, that smallest thing. Strange
that Asimov's book started
there, with something dying, then
moved to how people started
to believe in hell, and how the basket
Moses floated down the river in
was waterproofed, and a cross section of
what's under the ground, a cutaway
of a derrick and men standing near it
wearing hard hats, their bodies,
some showing confidence, some focus,

some obedience. I cited an owner's manual
for a 1979 Volkswagen van. I cited
an interview with my dad, dated
December 8, 1986. I wrote, *The whale*
oil supply was shrinking. I wrote about
bronze points and bamboo tubes
in China two thousand years ago. About
drilling for brine, for salt. *The whale oil*
supply, I wrote. First in a box
at my parents', then in a box in my
basement for years, this evidence
I was a good student, page numbers,
table of contents, everything printed
on a dot matrix printer and bound
with a plastic strip whose teeth curl
through a row of rectangular holes.

GEOGRAPHY V [1990]

The teacher who made us read *Anna Karenina*
also tried to tell us the earth
could open and take anything away.

One day after school I saw that plain-faced teacher
naked, unwrinkling a black swimsuit
up the dour rope of her torso. This gave me a horror

I kept for years: the faintness
clothing hides, her insignificant width.
The sag of skin unseen behind cloth.

She said her childhood neighbor was lost this way, and why
did the quake make the earth crack here
(the center of the calendar blotter on her wooden desk)
and not here (the edge of the blotter, near the stapler's jaw).
She said this comes to us all: One person survives

and another doesn't. That, and her rhythmic laps
in the black suit, polished with wet. Sallow arms
drew up, arched over; fingers reached toward
silence as she towed herself along, as though

each stroke were secret, and necessary, and must
not splash, and must not make a sound.

HISTORY I [1985]

We wanted caves, me and Carinne,
who was then Carrie, same as me. We
wanted what had never been seen, or
not seen in years. So much that we hid
old toys, hid notes in sandwich bags
under rocks, hoping to forget
and discover them later. Walking
the woods, imagined ourselves the first
to pass these cranberry shrubs—their
dank smell—and this fireweed—its fluff
clinging to our pale skin, then drifting off.
First to peel bark off this birch tree.

Carrie wouldn't stop talking
about the years her house was
the only one on the street. I wished
I'd been there to see it: instead of
the walls and carpets and roof I knew,
more woods, then soon a pit, one of
many, beside one of many mountains
of dug-up dirt. She laughed, talking
about it: *I was here! I saw it! Your house*
wasn't here! There was nothing! And her
remembering felt mean. Her delight
at holding within her life the start
of what we knew best. We knew
our ancestors were settlers. Did we see
that we were, too, some way, or
just after? Now, remembering, I'm
confused about old and new. What did
I want, and why? To have been
first? To see the past? To have
known the world before it was
the world? To know for sure
how thin? We lived in houses
so new it made no sound to walk

their floors. We had nothing
like the castles of Europe to visit, or
even an antique shop, or buried
bones. We knew about people
who wove baskets with willow, with
birch, but where were they? In our
bedroom closets, we built countries,
cut out and taped to the walls
pages from *Teen*—chose the heartthrobs
who looked softest, nearly as safe
as girls. We imported desk lamps, made
a language—for each letter
a new symbol. Took hours
to translate notes that never
gave any real news.

The weeks Carrie was grounded
for a C in math, I'd sneak to her
lower-level window. Across grass,
then across a field of cobbles, loose,
smooth, grey veined with white. I couldn't
walk to her window without
that jumble of hollow highness, those rocks
singing against each other.

ECONOMICS I [1985]

Would not exist without
oil is what I heard. We
wouldn't be here, I wouldn't
be here. Your body is made
of the parts of food, and food
comes from the store, and
it gets to the store by truck
and barge and those run
on gas, and to buy the food
we need money and how our
family makes money is Dad
goes to work in the glass-and-
metal building and his work
is getting oil out of the ground
and without that job we
would never have come here
and neither would so many
other people, there wouldn't even
be a store or the house that
some previous oil guy built and
lived in so our bodies are
made out of it really.
And how can you criticize
what you're made of, it's
like complaining about air.

GEOGRAPHY VIII [1993]

Some kids were stick pickers.
Drove the trucks all day
up and down the causeway
looking for trash, using those
long-handled tong tools
hopping out of the truck
to put it in bags. How even
to reckon. The tundra forever,
always wind, ocean, light, all summer

light and flare and the scientists
who checked to make sure nothing
at all had spilled into the river (called
fish squeezers, and some of them,
said Will, were all right). Hard hats
required outdoors. Earplugs
required. Gloves required almost
always. I have one photo

taken in the break room: four young people
in dark blue coveralls, in plastic
chairs at plastic tables. I've forgotten
all the names except Bridget and
Yves. Tall Styrofoam cups, half-pint
cartons of chocolate milk. On the wall,
a US map—five feet wide coast to coast
—and far southwest in the ocean,
palm-sized, the place we call Alaska.

ENGLISH IV [NOW (1987, 1993)]

On a day in May as I finished seventh grade
four barges floated away from New Iberia, Louisiana,
carrying every building I'd see on Endicott Island.
They floated to and through the Panama Canal
then hung a right and went about nine thousand miles
altogether—past Point Hope, Point Barrow. A sealift,
it was called, and it ended on an ice-free day
in August, when the barges reached the gravel
and people unloaded twenty-two thousand tons of
ready-made, equipment-filled buildings that would
click together to be the immaculate maze the oil runs
(after the rig and before the big pipeline) to be cleaned
of mud and water and gas, brought to temperature, to

pressure. So if you knew where they came from, even
saw them arrive, you couldn't help but call those buildings
forever and always *modules.* And if you arrived,
age nineteen, on a gravel island where people said
Be right back, just gotta run this out to Module 2 and
No smoking in the modules, ever and *Grab your hard hat*
and earplugs—we're going into the module, then *module*
would simply mean building full of pipelines, building that
thrums, building built for oil where not a drop of oil is ever seen.

LAW [1993]

The saying was, *A teacup*
is reportable. Meaning any liquid spilled
(besides water, and sometimes even
water), there was paperwork.
Forms that take time, said Randy.
That are a pain in the ass, said Will.
A teacup, as though most often
crude oil, or gritty citrus hand cleaner, or
yellow paint, or Simple Green solution
were held in teacups, might be
knocked over. As though on Endicott Island
or anywhere within hundreds of miles
instead of sixteen-ounce Styrofoam cups
for every meal there were teacups, as though
any of the giant-bellied men knew well
what it was to pick up a teacup,
to set it down. How much it would hold.
Set on a saucer, how it would sound.

SCIENCE FAIR III [1990]

One year it was fish and a chemical
common in plastic and the first step
was for my mother to drive me
to three, four different restaurants
where I'd ask a stranger/worker
if they please had any empty big
glass pickle jars I could please have
for my science fair project.
The deli came through with one
and a neighbor another in the name
of science. Somehow it was ok
that I bought from a fishery
some dozen one-inch salmon called *fry*
and gave half of them the chemical
in smallish doses. Chemical ordered
from a catalog that must have come
from Dad's office, ordered
by phone, which made me cry, first
not wanting to call, then hearing them
know I was young and small-voiced
and tell me, *No, you can't order that. It's*
a dangerous radiochemical. I was to—
but could not—*be brave* and finally
Dad called them and sorted out
my mix-up of names—told them
the one I needed was just *vanilla.*
A phrasing I remember. He said it—still
says it—like *vanella.* I still wonder
if that chemical—and I did wear gloves,
mostly, feeding it into the pickle jars
mixed with brown meal from
the cookie tin—will be the thing
that gives me the disease
that kills me. As it did the fish
who tipped as they swam for days

as if to show off a shine
(it was so important that I win
a ribbon) before they stopped and I
lifted them out with the little net.

HISTORY IV [NOW]

And we did get light—I believe it from
a podcast more than from my father's
mouth—from whale oil. And we took

baleen, took ivory, took lacquer
whose harvest kills a tree, took
tortoise shell. All soluble. All near

to soil. And now this pen will survive
me. These eyeglasses, these lenses,
these frames' light and dark stripe, irregular

as the shell of an animal who would float
among ocean waves—an animal seed,
fins slow as leaves—will survive me.

ENGLISH II [NOW]

Way back, when we said
something like *complicit,*
we meant *folded together.*
Even longer ago
we said *plek-* to mean
to plait. Also *complicate*
(to fold together). How we fold,
how we braid, when we bring
the tongue behind the teeth
behind the plosive lips: *exploit,*
imply, plight, replicate, pliant.

SOLUTION [1990]

One way was to try to be perfect.
Never let a Styrofoam cup cross
the counter into my hand. Make signs
on the backs of used papers to remind
the congregants to recycle. And then
with friends on Sundays meet at the door
and bag-brigade grocery sacks of wine bottles,
Diet Pepsi cans, beer bottles, newspapers,
newspapers, newspapers. Fill the little room
in the church basement until someone
shouted it was a fire hazard, until
we couldn't empty it except one bag at a time
to make a path to reach more bags. Shuttle
the Subaru and a friend's truck to a gravel lot
and heave each bag into the right bin. The next
week, all the same again. Same at school—

clear plastic bags, aluminum cans, unused
classroom, signs saying *recycle,* kids promising
they'd help empty the room next week, but
most of the time just me and Thomas Williams
(no relation) who wore a Greenpeace tee-shirt
most days and whose British accent meant his dad
was a big boss, carrying bags out the D-hall door,
dribbling Pepsi and chew spit. Teachers seeing us
and calling out thanks. Then at church for coffee hour

instead of disposable cups, ask everyone to bring
mugs to use, to wash, to reuse. And they did,
by boxes, rattling extras, enough for
twenty congregations' coffee, so many.

MUSIC I [1991]

It was the fashion to wear bangs tall and curled
up and back, hair blown out from the temples like wings,
a little like that guy in the ad for—what?—speakers?

The sound blows him away. What was the sound we
heard then? Walking in the morning to the bus stop without
a hat, ice that shattered over air, that skittered across

other ice. Some guitar. Some ice. Some news overlain
with static. Birch leaves. A voice saying how long it takes
lichen to grow. Skate blades sliding to a stop, a fan of ice, that spray.

ENGLISH I [1991]

The topic: What Petroleum Means
to Me. *Easy.* I wrote that oil is a rock
in the ocean, an island, firm, finite, full
of potential. That we take
and take from it to make our lives
go. That the island won't last. That we
should take less, or stop, find other
ways to power. And

I won. *They bought it,* I thought.
The point was *don't do it,* and the
Petroleum Wives in their sweaters
and nylons bought it, and the Wife
in charge of the contest handed me
a gold pan—a common trophy, flat bowl,
sloped sides, my name engraved
in the bottom along with *Winner,*
Petroleum Awareness Essay Contest.
Gold metal shaped like a tool you'd use
to hold and swirl wet gravel in a creek bed.
A way to sort out the useless rock
and make shining flecks show themselves.

I stood on the stage in the Captain Cook
ballroom and blushed and read what I wrote
for the crowd of oilmen's wives as they
touched their desserts with their forks.
The runner-up, a boy, shook my hand.
He said to me, *I used a metaphor too—holding*
your own bat. (Or maybe he said *bag?*) I tried
to look like I knew baseball, until he said, *Not relying*
on foreign oil. Maybe someone handed him
a gold pan too. Maybe we stepped
down from the stage together
then each turned from the other to choose
a path among the round tables.

HISTORY V [NOW]

Carinne left Anchorage, too, just a few years ago, and
last summer she went to visit. Saw her granddad, still living
at 100, and visited the child she calls her baby boy,

second son, drowned at seven. And her childhood house.
She said it hurt to see moss and lichen on the roof,
weeds shot up among those cobbles.

MUSIC II [NOW]

Here, too, among taller trees, I've seen
what we take. In one mine, a train
clattered down from humid, beyond-hot July
into a dry cool wind. Carts that might
rattle to pieces. In another mine,

a claptrap elevator box down and down,
about to collapse, rock layers flashing past,
wind cooling. Intruding: thought of the pounds
and tons of rock above, on top of us, our
small place to breathe. Minds' eyes
seeing it all, then closing, then unable to close.

In the largest cavern, a guide asks us to try
complete darkness, reminds us how rare
and, when no one objects, switches off
every lamp. Then, in a dark that was about
to become holy, he starts to sing, not well,
a story-song about men mining, a song
longer than anyone could want, not
in tune, way too much love in his voice
for their work, and we the dozen stand
through it with no way to walk away, no
way to even catch one another's eyes.

RESEARCH [2021]

I google Yves, the guy in that break-room photo who looked
like a sea god, whose mom was a white woman from
maybe Boston and whose dad was the mayor of maybe

the place we called Barrow. Yves talks on a podcast
about his town, now Utqiaġvik again, and I hear
for the first time that *g*, how it dwells in the soft

way-back of the throat, wide and dry. I hear
the *q*, shortest possible pop of connection
between tongue and palate. Now Yves

takes care of the sewer lines
as the permafrost melts and the ground
heaves and pipes buckle and break.

In 2020, off the clock, Yves flies a drone camera
over a whale camp. The water is black, the ice
white, snowed, whorled with sled tracks. People

are pushpins. At the edge of the ice, the whale
could be a long black fruit, a pear. Green ropes
are threads, taut from a post, tied to the tail,

like the body is ready to slide back into the sea, flesh
pendulum. A second whale has been skinned,
and red paths smear from the carcass

to a couple of orderly stacks of light pink.
In the soft snow, narrow walking tracks,
beside each other and on top of each other.

In Utqiaġvik, most of the sewer lines run through
a deep tunnel, heated, a system less expensive only than
the one on the space station. Yves

on the podcast says, *We've been really lucky*
with our oil money. We can afford to keep fixing them.

ART I [1985]

In spring, meltwater cut tunnels
under the snow berms. I wanted
to send my friend messages
by sealing notes in containers,
then floating them downstream. I had

a narrow glass vial with a plastic lid.
It had come in the mail—clipped to a card, full of
perfume—for my mom. I poured the perfume
down the bathroom sink, rinsed the vial.
What is that smell? said my mom.
Our plan had some problems. The vial

was too small to dry quickly, and
when I folded a tiny piece of paper
tightly and wedged it into the vial, it got wet.

Plus, the current wasn't always fast, so
to make the vial travel better I'd scoop water
from a puddle to sluice it down. For this
I stored a plastic bucket in a snowbank.
My mom noticed the bucket and moved it
to the garage, just to straighten things up.
When I protested, she suggested I leave
the bucket in the garage, get it out
when needed, use it, then put it away. This
vexed me. Do we store the phone receiver
in the garage until we want to make a call?

Besides, the vial could get stuck inside the tunnel,
or stall in an eddy. It was glass and therefore
breakable, its lid not watertight. And my friend

lived downhill from me and so, even if this worked,
wouldn't be able to write back. And what

to write? There was the phone. And she lived only
two houses away—why not just stand outside and yell?

GEOGRAPHY IX [1993]

At Endicott, my room was the mirror image
of the next room. Mirror, desk, bed.
Bathroom (shared). Bed, desk, mirror.

Four long corridors of rooms like that. Me
on the bed, journal open, pen, trying
to surprise myself, wondering how

I looked. Really looked. One room
was haunted. A man died there—
heart attack. People said he moved
in shadows, played with lights, flipped
the switch that locked one bathroom door
when the other opened. Randy said
not to talk about it—too scary—but
Will said, *That's just Hank.*
Hank's friendly. That summer I cried

a lot. I was dating a rude boy
who never called. I was so
righteous and so afraid. Outside,
across the gravel lot, a flame
on top of a metal tower,
jet roar all day, all night.
My dad now tells me

that can't be true. They never
flared that much, that long.
(The boyfriend would say
he called sometimes.)
After I heard about Hank,
my room felt haunted too.
I was so skinny my jeans
slid down my hips. For dinner
I only remember macaroni salad
with tuna and peas, cold, and sliced

melon, loving it. The money I made
would buy books, books I still own,
and ten-dollar pizza every time
I craved it, through the rest
of college. I wouldn't go back.

GEOGRAPHY IV [1990]

One teacher had just divorced
from a man my dad worked with.
She wore a sweater one day

thick and multicolored—
circles, triangles, squares, all
in different yarns, maybe some
metallic thread woven in and
borders crocheted around those
patches. I looked hard

at the sweater. The teacher
said, *At some point we all have to*
decide what to do about the fact

this sweater cost enough to feed
a family in Guatemala for months.
When class ended, all of us crowded

out the door, and a boy said,
not quietly, *Shitty sweater.*

PHYSICS II [1992]

I carried my cross-country skis out the door of the school
and that was ordinary. A trail all ascent and descent,
and that was ordinary. Where there were lights, the lights

were orange, and my shadow was blue and swung
around me, and the spruce a crowd of others
along the trail, and I was tooth-cold, throat-cold,

tight-skin cold until breath and glide, breath—glide.
Above a crest the high uninterrupted air. Below, gold
dim town and the inlet still and white, and as I tipped

into a fast downhill a deep brown living beast startled
out of the brush, carrying antlers, carrying body
of weight, and ran alongside my glide—I could have

touched its side, could hear exhales and smell
earth-scent, and dragged my poles and leaned
hard into one ski to keep away from the galloping

legs the heavy hooves gashing the snow, which were
beside me, then in front of me, then away into the thicket.

ASSIGNMENT [NOW]

How to hear a father say
I sacrificed and say
thank you. And
I reject it. And *I'm*
made of it and *stop*
and let no one else.

This and. This and knowing—
believing myself to know.

How did you raise someone
(give her every gift) how did you
raise someone who wants to
take apart what built her? How
to undo what's done us up?

At one time a living
is made. Was made for me. Milk
and whatever happened
I knew as the way. At one time

what I wanted most was
shine—a hairclip, sports-car
red, size of my fist, shaped
like a shell. A way to coat
every hair with varnish.

Some people voyage across
a sea and take a land
and then their great-
grandchildren are from
nowhere. One way is to
look for a small good. Loan
or give that man a twenty.
Buy her seagrass basket
even if you don't like it

and will never display it
on your living room wall. What
other ways. How to raise
ourselves to see what's
been done in our names.

TEST [NOW]

This is the way now. How
to crave an orange and eat
an orange and use that sugar
against—away. How, when we've
worked in its warehouse
and had our tuition paid?

Raise someone who could
look at you and say: *I'm*
never doing that. Of course, of
course you say back, *What*
else did you want me to—What
else could I have—How could
I have—I did my—

GEOGRAPHY VI [1992]

You could die by walking
onto the mudflats. By
disturbing the snow and being
rolled into an avalanche.
The snow would fill
your lungs. You could die by
walking in an alder thicket
without a bell, without
whistling or singing. From
leukemia, a little boy who played
hockey in a black-and-yellow
jersey. From climbing
onto the roof of a car dealership
to steal a huge balloon
as a prank—disturbing
the owner in his apartment
below. You could die

from the sun, from those
vacations you came home from
kissed by it every March, a braid
of colorful thread around one
lock of hair. The melanoma
already gaining on you while
every eye slid toward you, your
light steps along the lockered hall.

GEOGRAPHY VII [1992]

In the high school yearbook
a full-page article about kids
who'd hit moose with their cars.
One girl: *I cried. I kicked it and*
its antlers fell off. So gross.

I found my mom at the table
laughing tears onto this page.

What? I asked. *What is so funny?*
I never worked on the yearbook.
This whole article. Patted the page
with her hand. I had read it.

Was it funny? *I can't explain.*
Through laughter. *You'd never see this*
anyplace else.

ECONOMICS III [1989]

How many steps
between your family
and an oil well? The dollar
you bring for lunch
comes from a paycheck
from your mom, who
cuts the hair of the doctor
who repaired the lumbar spine
of the engineer flown in from
London to manage all of your
dads in their coveralls
or ties or coveralls over
ties. And your lunch. And so
your breakfast, Twix bar
bought with bills from babysitting
for the family who built
split-level wood-trim houses
on Klatt Road for the oil managers
and the secretaries and their plumbers
and realtors and interior
decorators. No sense
arguing with it, *hypocrite* always
ready to burn the veins. One way
was to succumb. Moose chili. Sheep
head on the wall. The glacier
we drove to every year, every
year farther across the bay.
We were new, so I knew
there was another way
and knew it was the same
way. Same but hidden—roads
and flights, our hunger
for citrus, for sweaters.
Lipstick. Blood mud
instead of frost but still
clotted, cup rim kissed.

PHYSICS I [1991]

As winter went on, the roadsides grew
steep with snow, and parking lots shrunk,
hemmed with berms. I rode the school bus,
every morning waiting in the cul-de-sac
with Christine, who took from behind a rock
her lighter and (now I get it) homemade
Diet Pepsi can bong to enjoy while we
waited. Kids who drove, most of them
drove trucks, and some boys had the idea
to park on snow berms in the school lot
the steeper the better. Front wheels up,
back wheels down. Or right wheels
four feet up on a snow pile, left wheels
low. So far nobody had thought to make
a rule about this. But one morning
after the pledge, the principal came on
and said she wanted to remind us all: Parking
was a privilege, and we were to park
between the lines, on the pavement. *No*
incline parking. Now it had a name. And

nobody had seen a painted line in the parking lot
since October. Who knew what was under
the three hard inches of snow-turned-ice?
Pavement? Grass? Something else? One boy
parked on the flat top of a six-foot snow pile
(technically not an incline). Others
stayed true to the slant. One April day,
the morning was frozen, but by noon
the sun turned snow to slush, and trucks sank
to their axles. After school, from everywhere,
the whine of wheels spinning, trying to back out.

ECONOMICS IV [1989]

About the time I learned to drive
I asked my dad why—
implying I couldn't imagine—
he took the job and kept it. The
pollution, the warming. We knew
then. We knew. *For you,*
I think he must have told me.
For your food and clothes
and so we can live.
Out the windows of my high school
every morning the Chugach Mountains
so near we were in them
sharp black next to sky sending up
purple-red. The hull of the *Valdez*
broke and gushed barrel
after barrel. The birds. Their
feathers. Surface coated thick. This
is why. I learned to pull the little latch
to open the gas cap door.
Pick up the handle, so much like
a goose face, hose neck—
to lift the lever, fill the car.

ECONOMICS II [1984]

One time the Petroleum Wives
had a picnic at McHugh Creek. I didn't want
to go, but we did, and their fingernails
red, eating at those wooden tables, talking
the kind of talk that bored even
my mom. Later that summer, or maybe
another summer, a bear killed someone
right there—an old woman jogging up the trail.

BIOLOGY [NOW]

Even though I've replaced
my cells one by one with
food bought with money taken
for grant writing, for copier
unjamming, for replacing
alot with *a lot,* for science, for adding
commas, for art, for the science
of knowing when it rained
millions of years ago even though
ok some help during the recession
and other times and at Christmas
a sweater, a jacket bought with
money earned at BP, my cells for
the most part rinsed by water from
other rivers, other taps, made
anew of labor put elsewhere—
even though copier, pen, ink,
lipstick, road to drive on
to the chosen job—even though.
Even though and still we still
depend and what could save still
could undo still rests on the
world made world too much like
our bones to dismantle even
still try to take it apart.

SCIENCE FAIR IV [NOW (1959)]

Over a jigsaw puzzle, my dad says,
One year I wanted to find out about
radiation, what it did, so I got a bunch of
fruit flies and put them in two big jars.
(My daughters listen while they sort
pieces.) *One of the jars I left alone, and*
one I brought to a dentist's office and
put it through the x-ray machine.

Mom says, *I'm surprised you were*
brave enough to do that. (He looks at her.)
Back then. (He keeps looking.) *You were*
shy. I want to know where he got
so many fruit flies, whether his parents
were ok with this, what size of jars, and
did the flies ever escape? He says, *I don't know*
how I got in touch with the dentist. I knew
his son, or someone did. His son drove me
across the bridge into Seattle. He was
rich. Well—his dad was a dentist, so
he was rich. Anyway, he had a nice car
and he drove me to his dad's office.

A jar of fruit flies is a jar of air, of places
to fly, is glass around a cloud of fruit flies.

My dad, a boy, held a jar of fruit flies
on his lap. My dad, a boy, carried the jar
from the car that impressed him
into the office, where he must have set it
on the chair where a patient would sit. *And*
what happened? I ask. *Did it kill them?*

He says, *It wasn't a good experiment. The glass*
absorbed most of the radiation, so they died

at the same time as the other ones. They died
when they would have already died anyway.

My dad, short for his age and shy, rides home
across that same bridge, a long bridge, low
to the water. My dad, a boy in the passenger
seat, doing the assignment, doing
science, holds the jar that holds the creatures
he thinks he's changed. My dad, a good boy,
watches the dentist's son drive that car away.
Carries the jar inside, sets it beside
the jar that's stayed in one place all along. Waits
to see what difference the trip made.

HISTORY II [1993]

And what does it mean, *in* my name?
As though a name, instead of
a word, were a kind of gas, a mist
among machines, like methane.

In the modules everyone had to carry
a sniffer. Little box on a belt loop
to pick up poison gases people couldn't
smell. Would sound the alarm. Somebody
said the sniffers could also smell farts,
and some boys tried all summer
to test that. A safety video showed a man

losing consciousness in a hole. Or was that
my dad's story years later of a man he knew?

Welders needed firewatchers. This, a student
could do: Stay awake, watch for sparks. Stay
awake. I never saw a caribou. Never saw
a fox. Once, in a village, my dad saw

a whale, hunted, people gridding it up
to eat for winter, trails of red footprints
where families carried away their shares.
Mostly he came and went, came and went,

a flight every week. In Anchorage we starved
for retail. The new mall had an ice rink
on the first floor, a pool underneath. Storefronts
that stayed empty until the next boom. On a spring
day, a gas leak filled the pool room, and someone
swimming laps stopped breathing. *Seventeen*
and *Sassy* came in the mail, and The Gap

seemed like it might exist
in New York but not here. Does vastness

ask to be chipped at? How do we raise
the question? At Thanksgiving? In the car?
In front of the TV? What do we raise? How
did you raise an animal who would growl
at you? A generation later
you could look and say *Who*
would build a world like this?

ART III [1993]

After work you could eat
dinner starting at 7. Work out
in a gym. A treadmill, I think,
some exercise bikes, a high
ceiling, maybe even skylights.
You weren't allowed outside
unless you had a reason. There was
no alcohol. Not in the modules, not
in the BOC, not in the shop,
a drive away anyway. You could die
carrying booze in winter in
the pocket of your thick
parka, in your truck, vodka
or rum still liquid but so cold a swig
could crack your esophagus,
is what people said. The rule
was firm. One night in the ten-seat
theater, we watched *Alive,* about
people whose plane crashed
in the mountains, how they took
one another's flesh as though
it were communion. The one who
did the cutting never told the others

whose meat it was. He saved them
from knowing if they were eating
a parent or a child. Some boys

stayed up to gorge on the midnight meal,
lunch for the night shift, then
slept all morning in the trucks,
radios off so no one could call them.

ESSAY [1983–NOW]

At the dinner table we learned, my brother and me,
the weeks our dad was home from the Slope, what *cog*
meant—a tooth in a wheel, like inside of a watch.

Watched his knuckles while he rolled together his two fists. That
was when another reorganization came up,
when it seemed he might or might not have a job next month.

Next month we might be asked to move to Pasadena (my mom
mimed vomiting) or Cleveland (she shut her mouth without smiling), or
Bogotá (her eyes closed). We heard about the price per barrel—

we learned you couldn't hit a barrel with a pair of wooden spoons
to make music. This barrel wasn't like a cup—it was more like an acre,
more like a mile per hour. Some things, we measure by pouring in,

pouring out. Some things, we measure as they go, at what
speed, through what, for how long, at what temperature, what
pressure. What we've lost, what we're losing, will lose. *Measure*

and *hold*—similar, but not the same. What we've done. Measure
or hold, or both? *Bring me a piece of paper,* he'd say, feeling
for the pen in his shirt pocket, *and I'll show you.* And an atom

would appear, the hard center of an atom, and its electron
cloud, or the way a guy named Zeno once talked about
movement: First go halfway, then half of the rest.

Half of the rest, then half of the rest. Will you ever
get there? Or a drawing that didn't help at all
of the twin who stays on earth and the one who travels.

The one who travels at the speed of light comes back unchanged.
How do you feel when you touch the plainest, cleanest thing
you know: a tee-shirt out of the dryer, or your coffee cup?

Your coffee cup in the morning: I'm telling you that's
exactly how it feels to be complicit, to benefit. I lay
on the floor figuring out my math homework, I'm saying.

I'm saying I watched *Three's Company* after school.
The permafrost is melting. The tundra does look (did look)
from the air like endless honeycomb, lines of water,

water that outlines fragments of earth. The land exists: flat
all the way to the horizon, its tufts of grass; flat
all the way out to sea along the grey; the constant light.

The light, and quickly the constant dark. While I think about this,
Facebook feeds me a story about a boss who fires a guy,
then sends his last paycheck in pennies, a wheelbarrow full—

pennies, a wheelbarrow full, coated in motor oil. Riddle:
What was the job? While I think about this, I read, *To go down*
into the earth is to travel back in time. I read that mining

has dragged the past into the present, has, on its way, changed
everything, out to the edge of the atmosphere. And while I think
about this, Facebook feeds me Ansel Adams, how his father,

rich from timber, gave him for his fourteenth birthday
two gifts—a camera and a trip to Yosemite. When I copy this story down,
I mistype *gifts* as *grifts.* While I think about this, I travel, as I do.

I travel, as I do every summer, with my husband and daughters,
by canoe across wilderness lakes, but where there used to be mud,
there's dust—dust on all the stems and leaves—

stems and leaves everywhere drained of green
and ready to crack, and one evening in hard wind a smoke plume
climbs the sky, and over a sleepless night orange flames breathe.

Orange flames breathe above the tops of the pines.
For a while, a friend says after we make it home, *I thought*
it might not affect us here. While I think about that,

I think about this: Two women sit on a dirt road on a hot day,
chained to a ladder, holding hands inside a length of pipe.
While I think about this, someone writes a letter.

A letter to the editor says those protestors couldn't have
gotten there without cars, without gas—*without pipelines*
they wouldn't have clothes or be able to eat.

Without pipelines they wouldn't have clothes or be
able to eat. Like there's no other way. Like that's the end
of the story, like *rely* and *fight* never lived in the same house.

In the same house, while I think about this, I read *Howards End*
and fall in love and partake. And I learn that as the tundra softens
what's been buried emerges: a preserved worm,

worm whose eggs thaw and hatch, whose offspring can't know
the twenty-four thousand years between mother
and grandmother. A mammoth body that, cut, bleeds.

Body that, cut, bleeds like a steak. What I do now, how I make
a living, is the smallest changes: a comma taken. Laid
and lay and lie. I remember the feed store in Anchorage,

the store where we went for guinea pig kibble and bales of
alfalfa. The fishing aisle, where a pair of waders
stood, bootsoles just above the floor, neoprene legs and torso,

torso up to shoulder straps, empty but surely
inhabited. I remember I dared to stay near it another minute
thinking of the tidal flats. I think about the story,

the story white people said Native people told,
and maybe they do, what have I ever learned, of a woman
whose lover was lost on a hunt, who wandered searching

and wandering, searching, lay down a moment, and fell asleep,
and the snow covered her until she was that mountain
on the horizon whose hair trails out behind her onto the land.

On this broken-promise land, how we really pay the bills is
a lake catches whatever's around it—pollen and leaves, dust and sand,
which settle, along with dying algae and little fish, to the lake's bottom,

and the lake's bottom, after millions of years, is made
of what's fallen, and what's fallen, we can pull up
in a cylinder, see in it the layers that mean cool, or warm, or no rain

or rain or more rain, and metaphor aside I've married someone
whose job is to look at those layers and say with clarity
that we've never been here before—this warm, this extreme,

this warm. This extreme. I've heard so much about the tar sands
in Alberta, what they call man camps, and the fracking boomtowns,
their tough, mean ways. But picture a place, picture

a place no more notable than an office in town, where
nobody can even buy a beer. See even the place I was closest
to crude, in the module, where the walls and ceiling,

the floors, the equipment, the pipelines were all painted
white and bright, scrubbed, shining. What if Moses's mother
hadn't had any pitch, nothing to use to waterproof?

With nothing to use to waterproof, how would any ark or basket
float, and who would have brought down those
stone commandments? I talk for the first time,

first time since 1992, with Thomas Williams, no relation,
who also hauled bags of pop cans out to Trevor's truck
to recycle, who also mainly remembers chew spit—

spit spilling out of cans, and teachers' thanks for all the good
we were doing, and he tells me how he feels when he
rinses out Ziploc bags and hangs them up to dry,

dries and reuses them, tells me *his* dad doesn't even believe
we are causing climate change. Says, with no anguish
at all, *I definitely live with a deep sense of hypocrisy.*

I definitely live with a deep sense of hypocrisy every day
of my life, and when I hear these easy words
I feel closer to home than I've been in a long time.

A long time after living near the place where it happens, I learn
whales travel a path in the deep, and for thousands of years
people reached them by camping on the ice shelf,

camping on the ice shelf far from shore, telling stories
and waiting for one to give herself. But now,
the ice unreliable, they make maps, or fly drones to see—

see the unreliable ice and make maps of cracks, see what's shifted,
where they might walk, what path might be solid—or else find
an unfrozen way wide enough to row or motor out to the open sea.

PHYSICS III [NOW]

Years later, my parents would say,
Remember when the moose
chased you along the ski trail? To chase

is to follow quickly, intending to catch
or to catch up. But the whole time,
the moose was in front of me or even
beside me. So I used to correct them:
It didn't chase me. It was more like I
chased the moose. And it might

have looked like chasing—both of us fast
along the same trail. But chasing
happens on purpose. The moose
chased me, or I chased the moose. Neither

is right, but I don't blame my parents or
myself for getting it wrong. We don't have
one word that means we both went
in an instant from startle to flee, got
pulled into gravity, a steep hill, narrow trail
free of trees but sheened with crisp ice
under powder. No one word means

we both had to ask, *What's the way*
out of this? Faster or slower? Neither of us
strong enough to stop. Each, I'm sure,
with a cold metal taste in the mouth.

ACKNOWLEDGMENTS

Thank you, Pádraig Ó Tuama, for choosing this manuscript and for your generous words.

I send this book into the world with gratitude for the places I've called home, and for the people whose work and care have sustained those places—and with gratitude for every person working daily, in large and small ways, for a planet in balance.

Thank you to the editors and readers of the following journals, where these poems first appeared (sometimes in different forms and sometimes with different titles):

Boxcar Poetry Review	"Geography V [1990]"
Rust + Moth	"History III [2018]"
The Iowa Review	"Economics IV [1989]" "Economics III [1984]" "English III [Now]"
Prairie Schooner	"English II [Now]" "History IV [Now]" "Music II [Now]"

Thank you, Molly Keenan, for your art.

Thank you to everyone at Wick Poetry Center, especially David Hassler, for your enthusiastic support of this book. Thank you, Kent State University Press team, for your careful work.

Thank you, Writing By Writers and Wolf House, for a week of quiet time in an inspiring space. Thank you, Andrea Cyr, for an affordable, sunny studio at a key time.

Thank you to the teachers—those who are in this book and those who helped me write this book: Deborah Keenan showed the way. Melanie Figg's Writing Hive provided structure and courage. Paula Cisewski offered playfulness, challenge, and community. b ferguson introduced a chorus of companions in the poetics of climate change.

For generous first (and second and more) reads and for insights, questions, interest, encouragement, and companionship, thank you, Naomi Cohn, Barbara Davis, Alice Duggan, Paige Riehl, Lia Rivamonte, and Hawona Sullivan Janzen; Michael Kleber-Diggs, Timothy Otte, and Lee Colin Thomas; and Kasey Jueds.

Thank you, Karlyn Coleman, Sara Dovre Wudali, and Anika Fajardo, for writerly friendship and sisterly magic.

Thank you, Anders, Ingrid, and Iris, for your constant support and love.

"English III [Now]" and "English II [Now]" draw on Etymonline's entries for *causeway, complicit, complicate,* and **plek-*.

Facts in "English IV [Now (1987, 1993)]" are from an August 1, 1987, story archived by UPI, "Barge Sealift Heralds First Arctic Offshore Oil Development," by Jeff Berliner.

"Research [2021]" refers to Alice Q. Glenn's interview with Yves Brower on the February 3, 2021, episode of the podcast *Coffee and Quaq.* It also references a photo by Brower published in the July 7, 2020, *High Country News* story "'What Choice Do We Have?,'" by Jenna Kunze and Kiliii Yüyan.

Whaling information mentioned in "Essay [1983–Now]" and alluded to elsewhere is from the aforementioned *High Country News* story and Kunze's "As the Arctic Warms, the Inupiat Adapt," in *High Country News,* July 1, 2020.

In "Essay [1983–Now]," the quoted line "To go down into the earth . . . " and the image of dragging the past into the present and into the atmosphere are Rebecca Solnit's, from *Orwell's Roses,* Viking, 2021; "bootsoles" belongs, of course, to Walt Whitman. That same poem contains the lines that began this collection, " . . . you couldn't hit a barrel with a pair of wooden spoons / to make music," which exist thanks to Elizabeth Alexander's "Praise Song for the Day."

www.ingramcontent.com/pod-product-compliance
Lightning Source LLC
LaVergne TN
LVHW100921110826
845155LV00035B/43
9781606355114